CATHEDRALS

CATHEDRALS

BY NEIL GRANT/ILLUSTRATED WITH PHOTOGRAPHS

◄—A FIRST BOOK—►

FRANKLIN WATTS, INC.
NEW YORK | 1972

(*Over*) *Detail from Reims cathedral in France.*
(MICHAEL HOLFORD, COURTESY OF
THE HAMLYN GROUP LIBRARY)

Cover design by Peter Bradford

SBN: 531-00755-3
Copyright © 1972 by Franklin Watts, Inc.
Library of Congress Catalog Card Number: 79-183939
Printed in the United States of America
1   2   3   4   5

CONTENTS

Every cathedral contains the throne of its bishop or archbishop. This is the throne of the archbishop of New York, in St. Patrick's Cathedral. It is used only on important occasions. (RELIGIOUS NEWS SERVICE PHOTO)

WHAT IS A CATHEDRAL?

The Greek word *cathedra* means a "seat" or "throne." A cathedral church (or "cathedral" for short) is a church that contains the throne of a bishop. The Roman Catholic religion, and some Protestant religions, too, are governed by bishops. It is a bishop who rules over a region, or diocese, each of which has its own cathedral.

The word "cathedral" is sometimes used to mean just a large church. But not every large church is a cathedral, and not every cathedral is a large building. St. Peter's in Rome, which is one of the most famous churches in the world, is not a cathedral. The throne of the pope (who is also bishop of Rome) is not in St. Peter's but in Saint John Lateran, a rather small church in Rome. Westminster Abbey, in London, is another famous church that is not a cathedral, although it was once, long ago.

A cathedral may be a large and splendid building, filled with rich art treasures, or it may be a simple wooden church in a poor country. Some cathedrals are a thousand years old. And some are being built at this moment.

In this book, we shall look at different kinds of cathedrals, as well as at some large churches that are not really cathedrals at all. We shall see cathedrals in Europe, in North America, and in Africa; rich cathedrals and poor ones; old ones and new ones. We shall even visit a cathedral that is still being built.

But although cathedrals are so varied, when someone says the word "cathedral" we think of a special kind of building.

The great Gothic cathedrals of Europe were built in the Middle Ages, over five hundred years ago. Many people believe that they are the finest buildings ever built anywhere. They are

1

certainly the most splendid products of the whole Middle Ages, which was the great age of cathedrals. Fine buildings have been erected since then, but nothing in Western architecture can compare with the Gothic cathedrals of Europe.

This book, then, is mainly about the medieval cathedrals of France, England, and Germany — how and why they were built and what has happened to them since.

THE FIRST CATHEDRALS

In the early years of Christianity, nearly two thousand years ago, the Church was not ruled by men. Its only ruler was God. The most important men were prophets and teachers, like the disciples of Jesus, who traveled from place to place.

As time went by, the affairs of the Church became increasingly complicated. Someone had to keep order and organize charities. Someone had to decide what services should be used in Christian worship. The Church needed a government.

In one way or another, the Church began to gain leaders. Sometimes, the leaders were elected by the people, and sometimes they were appointed by a famous prophet or teacher. At first, they were not very powerful. There was usually a group of them who shared their duties equally. Later, the duties were divided up, and each man had a special task. The head of each group was a bishop, and he was assisted by priests.

So each congregation had its rulers and its bishop, but there was still no ruler over all, except God. This caused difficulties. When two congregations disagreed, there was no one to judge between them. In the second century A.D. a new form of Christianity, called Gnosticism, nearly split the Christian Church in two. To guard against such dangers, the idea of "apostolic succession" was proclaimed.

According to this idea, the first bishops were the twelve apostles of Jesus. They had appointed others to succeed them and carry on their work. Bishops, therefore, were the direct successors of the apostles and the true guardians of Jesus' teaching. They alone could decide between true and false beliefs.

This idea made the bishops more powerful, but they did not always agree among themselves. They also needed a judge and a ruler.

The growth of Christianity increased the number of congregations under the control of each bishop, and some became more powerful than others. The first bishops had ruled only their own congregations. As their rule spread, they left each congregation under a priest, while they ruled a whole region, or diocese.

The most powerful bishops had their seat (or *cathedra*) in an important city, and they ruled a large diocese. They were called metropolitans (or archbishops). The most important of all was the bishop of Rome, which was the capital of the Roman Empire and the greatest city of the time. The bishop of Rome was regarded as successor of St. Peter, and he became the head of the Christian Church in the West.

Bishops wanted handsome cathedrals for their headquarters — the more powerful the bishop, the larger the cathedral. The first cathedrals, however, were rather small wooden structures. Timber was plentiful, and wood was easier to work with than stone. But wooden buildings decay and burn easily, and none of those early cathedrals lasted very long.

Cathedrals soon became grander, and were built of stone instead of wood. Although stone buildings stood up well to thunderstorms, battles, and fires, only a few ruins of the earliest stone cathedrals are left.

One reason for their disappearance is that they were often rebuilt. As a town grew rich, or its bishop became more powerful, the old building did not seem grand enough, so it was torn down to make room for something more splendid.

In many old towns in Europe, archaeologists have followed this rebuilding process through many centuries. Their discoveries are often made by chance. Perhaps it becomes necessary to repair the foundations of a cathedral, and when the digging is under way, the repairmen find the remains of an older building which no one knew about. A little more careful digging, and the remains of yet another building are revealed, older still. In the deepest part they may find the traces of ancient wooden beams, all that remains of the first church ever built on that spot. The history of European cathedrals goes back much further than the buildings we see today.

There is an example of such an old site in Chichester, England. Chichester cathedral was nearly destroyed a hundred years ago when its spire collapsed and fell onto the roof. During the repairs, the builders had to dig into the foundations. About

Cathedrals in Europe were built in the center of large towns, with houses crowding round them. Strasbourg cathedral towers above the town like a giant standing among dwarfs. (FRENCH GOVERNMENT TOURIST OFFICE)

6

eight feet below the floor of the cathedral, they found a Roman mosaic floor in quite good condition. Chichester cathedral is one of the oldest in England, but this Roman floor may have been there five hundred years before the cathedral was built, perhaps even before England became Christian.

The cathedral authorities in Chichester have left a hole in the floor, so that visitors can see the Roman work just as the builders discovered it.

During the sixth century, an important development took place in the Christian Church. This was the beginning of the age of the monasteries. Monks and abbots are clergymen, but unlike priests and bishops, they do not live among ordinary people. They live in monasteries, and their life is governed by strict rules. The building of monasteries had an important effect on cathedral-building, and many of the greatest cathedral builders were monks.

In Europe, the cathedral system and the monastery system were separate. But in England, monasteries and cathedrals were sometimes combined. Christianity did not arrive in England until the monastery system had already started. In fact it was a monk, St. Augustine, who brought Christianity to England. Some cathedrals were built with a monastery attached, and they were run by monks instead of ordinary priests. Now we shall see how a cathedral-monastery was founded in Norwich, England.

Abbeys or monasteries were built far away from the bustling towns, so the monks could pray and study in peace. This is the abbey of Mont-Saint-Michel in France, which is cut off by the sea at high tide. The houses were built at a later date. (FRENCH GOVERNMENT TOURIST OFFICE)

THE GREAT AGE
OF CATHEDRAL-BUILDING

Early in the Middle Ages, the Christian Church went through a long, dark period. It began to revive in the eleventh century. Pope Gregory VII, one of the greatest leaders the Church has ever had, renewed the power of the papacy. The rule of the pope, said Gregory, was greater than the rule of kings and princes, and greater than the rule of the Holy Roman Emperor himself.

It was an age of strong religious feeling. Priests and monks became more active. People everywhere in Europe wanted to show their love and fear of God by building great churches.

At the same time, Europe was becoming more prosperous. Trade was increasing and towns were growing larger. There was more money to spend on building.

So the great age of cathedral-building began.

The style of architecture in Europe during the eleventh century is called Romanesque, because it is like the style used in ancient Rome. It is easy to recognize a Romanesque building by its round arches, which are exactly the shape of a half-circle. The round arch was invented by the Romans. In the eleventh century, no one had yet invented a better way of supporting the vault (a curved, stone ceiling) of a large building.

The Roman style was very strong. It is no accident that many buildings of the ancient Romans, as well as many Romanesque ones, are still standing today.

Romanesque cathedrals, like those at Angoulême or Worms, look solid and powerful. Inside, they are dark and rather narrow. They seem to tell us something about the religion of the

The Romanesque style lasted longer in Germany than in France. This is the cathedral of Worms, in Germany, built in the twelfth century. Notice the rounded windows and arches, and the heavy, solid look of the whole building. (ROGER VIOLLET)

men who built them. The medieval Christian Church was as powerful and unchanging as its buildings, and the faith of the people was strong, but narrow.

But the Romanesque style had some serious drawbacks. The round arch is strong, but it is also heavy. The walls or columns that it rests on must be extremely thick. Also, the height of the arch cannot be more than half its width. So Romanesque churches have to be narrow, with huge columns to support the vault. The higher the vault, the thicker the columns. Walls must be thick and strong or they will be forced outward. This means that windows have to be small, to avoid weakening the walls.

Romanesque buildings used a large quantity of stone, which sometimes had to be brought from far away. The great expense of transporting the stone was another reason why the Romanesque style was unsatisfactory.

Romanesque and Gothic arches. The arrows show how the arches pressed on their supports. A Romanesque arch presses down and outward. A Gothic arch presses almost straight down, so that the ground bears more of the weight.

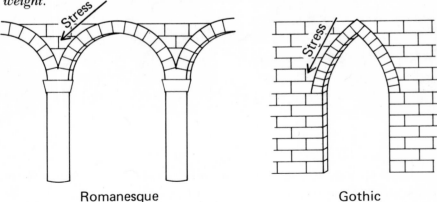

Romanesque   Gothic

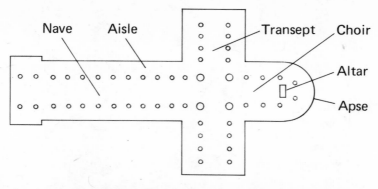

A simple plan of a cathedral, which shows how it was built in the shape of a cross. Of course, every cathedral was different, and not all were cross-shaped. Usually, chapels were built on around the east end.

During the twelfth century, a great discovery was made: an arch need not be round; it can be pointed! This was the most important discovery in architecture since the days of ancient Rome, but nobody knows who made it. Probably, the idea was brought back from the East by Crusaders returning from the Holy Land.

The new style was called Gothic (the Goths were a German people, but they did not invent the Gothic style, so it is not a very appropriate name). Just as the round arch is the mark of Romanesque architecture, so the pointed arch is the mark of Gothic.

The chief advantage of a pointed arch is that it puts less strain on the walls or columns. Whereas a round arch presses outward, a pointed arch presses almost straight down. Walls and columns can be thinner. Less stone is needed, and building is therefore cheaper.

The pointed arch allowed other improvements, too. The vault could be raised higher and, because the walls did not have to be so strong, large windows could be used. Great windows of stained glass are another mark of the Gothic cathedral.

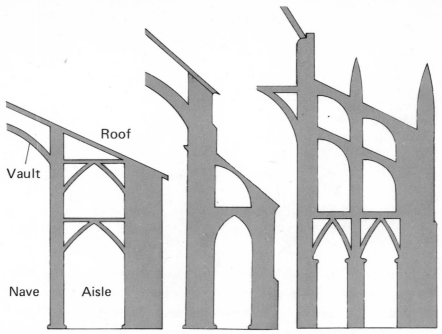

Roof

Vault

Nave   Aisle

These three drawings show how the flying buttress developed. As time went by, it became more elaborate, and "flew" across wider spaces.

Medieval architects soon worked out a way to reduce the strain on the walls even more. They constructed stone ribs that crossed the vault at an angle and carried the weight of the vault to certain points in the walls. At these points, the wall was strengthened with projections, or buttresses.

The true Gothic style lasted for about three hundred years, but of course it did not always remain the same. Changes and improvements were made throughout that time. One of the most interesting was the development of the buttress.

The first buttresses were simply an extra thickness of wall at the point where it was joined by the ribs from the vault. As time went by and cathedrals grew larger, the buttresses increased in size. They supported almost the whole weight of the vault, and the actual walls had little work to do.

Soon, buttresses were only attached to the wall at one point, near the roof. They were like large pillars, joined to the main building by a sweeping shaft of stone. They are called "flying buttresses," a very good name, because they do seem to "fly" out from the walls, carrying the weight of the vault, through the pillar, to the ground. The flying buttress was the finest invention of medieval architecture after the pointed arch.

The Gothic style belongs mainly to northern Europe. In the sunnier south, buildings with large windows were not needed; it was more important for a building to be cool than light.

Many of England's finest cathedrals are Gothic, and Germany, too, has fine Gothic cathedrals. But the most splendid of all are to be seen in the Ile-de-France, the region around Paris. It was here that the Gothic cathedral, with its gracefully pointed arches, beautiful stained-glass windows, and breathtaking flying buttresses, had its true home.

HOW ONE CATHEDRAL WAS BUILT

A traveler who approaches the English city of Norwich from the west sees the graceful spire of the cathedral rising high above the buildings. Even today, when office and apartment buildings rise higher every year, Norwich cathedral still dominates the city. Five hundred years ago, it seemed even larger.

Norwich then was a rich market town, one of the three largest towns in England. But to us, it would not have seemed much larger than a big village. The houses were small and built

13

Norwich cathedral (England) from the south. The long nave was not built in the time of Bishop Herbert de Losinga. Nor was the tower with its spire on top. (A. F. KERSTING)

of wood. The whole population could have stood inside the cathedral. Imagine New York's Empire State Building in a midwestern town. The cathedral towered over medieval Norwich in much the same way.

How did such a huge and complicated building come to be built? Who was the man who designed it? Where did the thousands of tons of stone come from? Who were the workers, and who paid the cost?

We cannot answer all these questions. It is nearly nine hundred years since Norwich cathedral was begun, and part of the story is lost. We do not know the name of the master mason — the man who was in charge of the work of building. We do not know who drew up the plan, or if there was a plan at all.

But we do know the man who founded the cathedral: Herbert de Losinga, the first bishop of Norwich. It was through his ambition and energy that this splendid building was raised on a marshy English field.

Herbert de Losinga was not an Englishman. He was born in France, and was invited to England in 1087 by King William II, who was his friend. The king made him abbot of Ramsey, although the monks of Ramsey were not pleased to have a foreigner appointed to rule them.

In those days, the Church was richer and more powerful than it is today. Bishops and abbots were important figures; they were politicians — even soldiers — as well as priests. Talented men who were not born rich became priests because that was the only way to gain money and power. Herbert de Losinga was one such man. Although he was religious, he was also ambitious and fond of power. He felt just as much at home in the king's court as in a monastery.

In 1091 the bishop of Thetford died. Herbert wanted the job, and to get it he paid the king a large sum of money. This was a sinful way to get a promotion, but it was not an uncommon one.

Thetford was not so large as Norwich, and its cathedral was rather small. The policy of the Norman kings was to build large cathedrals in large towns. So Herbert decided to move his seat to Norwich, where he would build a new cathedral with a monastery attached to it.

Money was the first problem. Herbert was a good businessman, and he was already a rich man, but not rich enough to pay for his cathedral. The king gave land for the site, but he had recently quarreled with Herbert and that was about the extent of his contribution. Neighboring barons gave some help, and in 1096 Herbert himself laid the first stone.

Work began at the east end of the cathedral, where an old church was pulled down to clear the site. The insides of the walls could be filled with ordinary rocks, but the surfaces required stone of better quality. Because there were no stone quarries near Norwich, the stone had to be brought from far away. Some of it came from a quarry in central England, and some came from Caen, in France. It was brought by ships, which sailed around the coast and up the river that ran close by.

The work was directed by the architect, or master mason. He had his own gang of men, skilled workers who traveled with him from one job to the next. But many of the workers were

This strange statue comes from above the north door of Norwich cathedral. Experts believe it is supposed to be Herbert de Losinga. Probably, it once covered his tomb. (NEIL GRANT)

monks and the servants of the bishop. The king also sent some of his servants to help.

It seems that the monks did not always work hard. The energetic bishop wrote them a sharp letter: "The king's servants and mine," he wrote, "do their work well, but you sit around half-asleep, as if your hands were paralysed."

Herbert was often away on business, trying to raise more money for his cathedral. While he was away, he sent many letters to his people in Norwich, urging them to greater efforts. In 1101, enough of the cathedral had been built to hold services regularly. From that day to this, Christian services have been held every week in Norwich cathedral.

Herbert de Losinga died in 1119, aged about sixty-seven. His cathedral was still far from finished. The eastern part, with its curved chapels and wide aisles, was complete. But the tower had risen no higher than the roof, and the long nave, or central hall, had hardly been started.

Today, Norwich cathedral looks very different from the building that Herbert dreamed of. He began it in the Roman-esque (or Norman) style, but the parts that were added later were built in the style that was fashionable then. The present spire was built in the fifteenth century, after an earlier one had fallen down. But without the energy and ambition of Herbert de Losinga, the cathedral might never have been started.

The shortage of money was especially serious in Norwich, but other cathedrals had the same kinds of problems. To bring about their amazing achievements, the cathedral builders were necessarily men of strong determination and deep religious faith. Fortunately, there were others like Herbert de Losinga, whose work remains for us to admire today.

THE WORK OF A CATHEDRAL

The cathedral was the biggest building in a medieval city. It was also the *only* public building. It was used for many purposes besides religious services. The poor and the sick were cared for in the cellars (called the crypt); citizens gathered in the aisles to conduct business.

The New Testament tells us how Jesus angrily drove the money changers out of the temple in Jerusalem. He would have found the same kind of work to do in a medieval cathedral.

If you go into a cathedral in Europe today, the building is probably quiet and empty. The great stone columns soar majestically toward the high roof. Light comes dimly through the stained-glass windows. Your footsteps echo around the ancient walls, and you feel you ought to speak in a whisper.

Five hundred years ago, the scene was quite different. The place was buzzing with noise. Merchants displayed their goods on a table in the nave, or they set up a stall in the churchyard outside. Farmers stored grain in the galleries and wine in the cellars because the cathedral was safer than a wooden barn. Sometimes, the grain was actually ground, and beer was brewed, inside the cathedral. A few reminders of all this can still be seen today. For example, carved in the wall of the cathedral at Freiburg in Germany, there is a table of weights and measures, which merchants once used for measuring their goods. At other places, stalls for selling books or even food can still be seen clustered against the cathedral walls.

Medieval churches gave shelter not only to the poor and the sick, but also to criminals on the run. The right of sanctuary promised that a man who took shelter in a church could not be

One of the horrible heads that medieval craftsmen liked to carve on cathedral gutters. Rainwater drained through its mouth and was thrown clear of the walls. (FRENCH GOVERNMENT TOURIST OFFICE)

arrested. It was a serious matter whenever the right was broken. When Archbishop Thomas Becket was murdered in Canterbury cathedral by servants of King Henry II, all Europe was shocked by the deed. To show his sorrow, the king, barefooted and wearing rough clothes, made a pilgrimage to Canterbury and allowed the monks to beat him with whips.

Religious services were held daily in the cathedral. Even then the noise did not stop, for people went on discussing their business in the aisles. Anyway, the service was said in Latin, which only priests could understand.

Life in the Middle Ages was hard and dangerous. The people worshiped a stern god. When the plague killed a whole town, men believed that it was an act of God, who punished all sinners. For the people of the Middle Ages, hell was a real place, where sinners were punished in horrible ways.

Imagine that you are standing near a medieval cathedral, looking at its splendid towers, sweeping arches, and glorious windows. Now look a little more closely at the pictures in the windows and the carvings around the doors. Here are strange figures that are not at all grand or glorious. Devilish creatures, with faces carved on their stomachs and carrying spikes, are driving sinners into hell. Hell is pictured as a huge mouth with sharp teeth. Flames are roaring up into its throat.

This scene is on the magnificent cathedral of Bourges, in France. But scenes like it can be found on all medieval cathedrals. At the ends of the gutters, which carry rainwater from the roof, are carved heads. The water pours out from their mouths. These heads, which are called gargoyles, are often extremely ugly. Some are funny, but some are really frightening.

Or look under the tip-up wooden seats in the choir. In monastery churches, like Norwich cathedral, these seats have a ledge that monks could lean on when they had to stand for a long time during the services. Below the ledges are lively wooden carvings of scenes from medieval life. A schoolmaster is beating a lazy pupil. An old woman is chasing a cow. Or a fox, dressed in the clothes of a monk, is being hanged on a gallows (monks were often unpopular).

Sometimes, the designs in stained-glass windows also show scenes that are not at all religious. They may be pictures of ordinary life — peasants sowing their seed, or treading grapes into wine. Or they may show some strange and mysterious happening.

In a window of Lyons cathedral, a peculiar bird is standing on a man's chest. A carving in Notre Dame cathedral in Paris, shows two hands holding a box. In Amiens, there are scenes carved in stone that look like an early cartoon strip. One picture shows some men setting fire to a harbor. The next picture shows three men, with crowns on their heads, sailing away from the burning harbor.

What do all these strange things mean? Although they are mysteries to us, they were not created to be mysterious. The men who carved them were simple craftsmen who often could not read or write. This is a clue. Not many people in the Middle Ages *could* read or write. But they could learn from pictures, and the pictures in churches were intended to teach them. The ship sailing away from the burning harbor tells the story of King Herod, who ordered the ships at Tyre to be burned when he was trying to capture the Three Wise Men. But, as the next picture explains, the Three Wise Men managed to escape in time.

The towers of Laon cathedral, in France, with the famous oxen looking out over the town. These stone animals were made in memory of the oxen that carried the building stone to the cathedral in the twelfth century. (MICHAEL HOLFORD, COURTESY OF THE HAMLYN GROUP LIBRARY)

Those horrible gargoyles on the outside warned passersby that devils and evil spirits would catch them if they did not obey the Church. The scenes of peasants sowing and harvesting reminded people that they must lead an honest, hardworking life if they wanted to go to heaven.

Medieval people were superstitious. For example, although they were Christians, they also believed in witchcraft. The priests encouraged their superstitions, because while the people lived in fear, the Church had more power over them.

Every simple act had a religious meaning. A workman carrying firewood thought of Christ carrying the cross. Men believed that the bird called the crossbill got its twisted beak from trying to pull the nails out of the cross. A monk, cutting up an apple, divided it into three parts in memory of the Trinity (God the Father, God the Son, and God the Holy Spirit).

The very stones of the cathedral had a message for the worshipers. Cathedrals usually had three doors at the west end. People believed that this too was a sign of the Trinity. Then, most cathedrals were built in the shape of a cross, which people thought was a sign of the cross on which Jesus was crucified. They did not know that the first cathedrals were oblong. Projecting transepts, which cause the cross shape, were first added for a very simple reason — to make more room inside! They had no religious meaning.

Toward the end of the Middle Ages, cathedrals ceased to be the center of town life. During the Reformation, half of Europe became Protestant, and some Protestants did not like cathedrals. They were too grand and too rich for people who believed that religion should be simple.

The Christian religion itself became unpopular in some

places during the seventeenth and eighteenth centuries. This was the "age of reason" in France, when men like Voltaire attacked Christianity as a superstition, no better than witchcraft. The magnificent old abbey church of Cluny was blown up, and its stones used for new buildings. The cathedral of Tours was turned into a stable for horses. In republican Paris, the cathedral was offered for sale.

In the twentieth century, most people believe that cathedrals should be cared for, because they are old and beautiful. Yet cathedrals have suffered more damage in this century than in any earlier time. For one thing, Gothic cathedrals are growing older. Stones crumble, walls crack, and foundations sink. No building lasts forever without repairs, and repairing a Gothic cathedral can be very expensive. All the same, these ancient buildings are amazingly strong. The architects of the Middle Ages could not foresee bombs and heavy artillery, or air pollution. Yet many of their buildings have survived through years of vandalism, wars, and smog.

ABBOT SUGER
AND THE GOTHIC STYLE

In 1137, Abbot Suger began to rebuild the abbey of Saint-Denis, just outside Paris, France. The work lasted for twelve years, and the result was the first Gothic building.

Suger was an extraordinary man. His parents were poor, and he became a monk as a young man. It was difficult at that time for a man of humble birth to go far in the world, yet Suger rose to the greatest position in France. Not only was he abbot of Saint-Denis, the royal church of France, but when King Louis VII was away on a Crusade in the East, Suger was made the ruler of the kingdom.

The new abbey was to be a place of *light*. Jesus Christ was "the true Light" and he "lighted men's souls." These words had real meaning for Suger. Light, he believed, was the sign of God's love for man. So he insisted on large glass windows and slender columns to let the light into his abbey. Gothic art has since then been called the "poetry of light," a description that Abbot Suger surely would have liked.

Suger's work at Saint-Denis was limited by the presence of the old abbey, which could not be pulled down because it was too holy. According to legend, Christ himself had appeared at the time of its dedication.

There were other difficulties, too. Everyone said that there were no trees in the region large enough to supply the twelve enormous beams needed to support the roof during the rebuilding. As Abbot Suger lay in bed one night, thinking about this problem, he decided he would look for the trees himself. Next day, with a band of workmen, he set off into the forest. The local gamekeepers just smiled when he described the size of the trees he needed. Impossible! But the abbot did not give up. He told his men to spread out through the woods and to search for eight hours. To their surprise, when they gathered together, they had found, between them, exactly twelve suitable trees. To Suger, it was the work of God.

The Gothic style did not suddenly replace Romanesque.

The change came about slowly, and in some places it never happened at all. Early Gothic cathedrals have many Romanesque features, and some buildings were designed in the Romanesque style long after the Gothic age had begun. Nevertheless, we can see that Suger's work marks a dramatic change.

The abbey of Saint-Denis was the signal for a great outburst of cathedral-building in the Ile-de-France. During the next two centuries, nearly every town in this region was building new churches or cathedrals.

These towns were small places (only Paris had more than ten thousand people). They were surrounded by a wall, and the houses were built close together. The cathedral was usually in the center of the town. It rose suddenly from the mass of buildings and towered over the roofs of the homes that pressed against it.

Although medieval builders had no heavy machinery, the construction site was a noisy — and untidy — place. Against the rising walls of the cathedral were sheds for the workmen. Carts went back and forth, bringing stone from the quarries. Carpenters put up wooden scaffolding. Stonecutters chipped away with hammers and iron chisels. Mortarmen mixed cement for binding the stone blocks together. Laborers turned a wheel that worked the pulley, hauling stones up to the top of the walls. A mason's assistant hung a weighted string (called a plumb line) from the top of the wall, to make sure it was straight.

Somewhere nearby, perhaps inside the building, a square of plaster was laid on the ground. Here stood a man with expensive clothes and clean hands, carrying a pair of dividers for measuring distances and angles. He drew lines in the plaster with a pointed stick. Sometimes he spoke to the workmen, who treated him with respect, for this was the master mason, the architect of the cathedral.

Parchment (a kind of paper made from animal skin) was very expensive. So architects usually scratched their designs in plaster or on stone. In a few places, such as Wells cathedral in England, the remains of the architect's drawings can still be seen. But no complete plans have survived. It is a pity that we have so few records of the work of the medieval architects. Even the names of many of them are lost.

THE GUARDIAN OF PARIS

Most of the French cathedrals that were begun in the late twelfth century were dedicated to "Notre Dame," which means "Our Lady" (the mother of Jesus). But when someone talks about "the cathedral of Notre Dame," we know at once which cathedral he means. He means the cathedral of Paris, the most famous of all French Gothic cathedrals.

Notre Dame stands on an island in the Seine River, in the center of France's capital city. For eight hundred years this little island and its cathedral have been at the heart of French history.

Notre Dame of Paris, from the east. Notice the high, curved apse and the flying buttresses. With its slender wooden spire, like a mast, the cathedral made people think of a large ship. (MICHAEL HOLFORD, COURTESY OF THE HAMLYN GROUP LIBRARY)

They have been the scene of many great events, some splendid and some terrible. In this chapter, we shall travel quickly through those eight hundred years and look at some of the triumphs and disasters of Notre Dame.

Paris cathedral, like many others, stands on an ancient religious site. There were at least two Christian churches here before Notre Dame was built. The first one appeared as early as the fourth century. Before that, the site was occupied by a temple to the Roman god Jupiter. Its altar can still be seen in a Paris museum. Even earlier, strange Celtic gods were probably worshiped here by people dressed in animal skins. Long before people began to record history, the island was a center of religion.

The cornerstone of the present cathedral was laid in 1163 by Pope Alexander III. For a time, construction was swift. The main body of the cathedral was finished in only sixty-one years. That was rapid progress for such an extraordinary building. For Paris was the first cathedral to have fully developed flying buttresses. And because it has a double row of aisles, the buttresses have to leap across an extra-wide space. From the east, the cathedral looks like a ship, its buttresses springing out like great oars, advancing along the Seine.

The whole building was finished, except for a few small details, in about one hundred and fifty years. It was one of the few Gothic cathedrals to be completely finished before the end of the true Gothic age.

In its early years, Notre Dame was the center of Paris life. It was a house for people as well as a house of God. Those who had nowhere else to sleep could spend the night in the cathedral. Slaves were given their freedom in it, and hunted men found sanctuary there. Knights took the Crusader's oath at the altar, before they set out to recapture Jerusalem from the Muslims.

Travelers came to show the strange objects they had brought from foreign lands. Ostrich eggs, elephant tusks, and even stuffed crocodiles could be seen in Notre Dame. Market stalls were set up, and simple plays were performed in the nave by traveling actors. Outside, the citizens would throw rotten fruit at criminals in the stocks.

In Notre Dame, Henry VI of England was crowned king of France, when he was a boy of ten. Soon afterward, Joan of Arc appeared on the scene to send the English packing.

Flags that were captured in this and other wars were hung in the cathedral. They looked splendid, but they were a fire hazard. One day, a thief was hiding in the roof, hoping to steal the silver candlesticks from the altar. At night, he let down a rope to pull them up to his hiding place. But the candles were alight. They brushed against the dusty old flags, and in a few minutes, the cathedral was filled with flames and smoke.

In later times, Notre Dame suffered much worse disasters. In 1699 some alterations were made by a famous architect. He was the designer of a beautiful square, the Place Vendôme in Paris, but he had no love for the old Gothic style. He destroyed the altar, the stalls (seats), and many medieval carvings. He covered the columns with ugly marble slabs and spoiled some of the old tombs.

A few years later, it was decided that the cathedral was too dark. Along came some workmen with hammers. They smashed the priceless, stained-glass windows and put in plain glass instead.

The eighteenth century was a terrible time for the cathe-

dral. Strangely, most of the damage was done by good and sincere men. They did not understand the value of the things they destroyed.

In 1789, the French Revolution broke out. Both religion and royalty became very unpopular. Statues of French kings in the cathedral were taken away. Rioting mobs ran through the building, destroying sculptures and breaking glass. The revolutionary government renamed the ancient cathedral a "Temple of Reason," and an actress was crowned "Goddess of Reason" on the High Altar.

The worst insult of all was still to come. The cathedral was put up for auction. It was bought by a man who wanted to knock it down and use the stone for new buildings. Just in time, Napoleon came to power and Notre Dame was saved.

In 1804, Napoleon was crowned emperor by the pope. On that day the cathedral regained its old glory. But it was still in a sad state, with nearly all its art treasures stolen or destroyed and its walls scarred and broken.

Between 1845 and 1860, the cathedral was restored by a famous architect named Viollet-le-Duc. He was a man of strong will and great energy, a lover of the Gothic style, and a famous scholar of medieval architecture. His aim was to make the cathedral look exactly as its medieval builders planned it. It was a difficult and expensive task. Not everyone admired his work. Some said that he did his job "too well," because he introduced

The square west end of Paris cathedral gives it a look of strength and power. A "gallery of kings" runs across the whole front. Notice that there are eight statues below the north tower but only seven below the south tower. This happened because the south (right-hand) tower is narrower than the north. (A. F. KERSTING)

33

some "improvements" that the medieval builders never thought of. But this was rather unfair, for Viollet-le-Duc did a splendid job. Even the gargoyles were carefully replaced. Everyone who visits Notre Dame owes him a debt of gratitude.

The story of Notre Dame is not very unusual. Other old buildings were treated just as badly, especially during the seventeenth and eighteenth centuries.

Perhaps we can learn a lesson from their troubled history. Styles and fashions change with time. Buildings (or any other objects) that we do not like may one day be loved and respected by our descendants, and we should be careful not to destroy the treasures of the future.

WHERE KINGS WERE CROWNED

During the great age of cathedral-building in France between 1150 and 1250, every town tried to outdo its rivals. Each new cathedral had to be larger or grander than all the others. For example, the height of the choir (the section usually occupied by the singers and clergy) steadily increased. Laon cathedral, begun about 1160, had the highest choir at that date. Paris, begun in 1163, beat Laon with a vault that was 115 feet above the floor. Chartres, in 1194, raised the record to 120 feet. The cathedral of Reims, begun in 1211, followed that with 124 feet; and Amiens, begun in 1220, leaped to 139 feet.

Finally, the medieval builders reached the limit. The choir of Beauvais cathedral rose to the amazing height of 157 feet, 3

The amazing cathedral of Beauvais, which was never finished, is the tallest of French cathedrals. (ROGER VIOLLET)

inches. A building of fourteen floors could have been erected inside it without touching the vault.

But the citizens of Beauvais did not enjoy their success for long. In 1284, only twelve years after the choir was built, the walls began to bend outward. The roof sagged and, with a terrific crash, it tumbled to the floor below.

This disaster did not end the ambitions of Beauvais. Nearly three hundred years later, a huge spire was erected. At that time, the nave (which in a Gothic cathedral helps to support the spire) had not yet been finished. The money for building it had been used to repair the choir. For a few years the lofty spire rose high into the sky, then, without warning, it tilted, cracked, and fell in ruins.

Once more, the choir had to be rebuilt. But the cathedral never was finished. It stands today, a massive and splendid block in the center of the town. It is a memorial to the high ambitions of its builders. And some people feel that this crippled giant is more wonderful than the completed building could have been.

Every tourist has his own favorite among the cathedrals of northern France. Notre Dame of Paris has the most interesting history. Chartres has a deep religious atmosphere that no other cathedral can equal. The sheer size of Amiens makes it especially impressive.

Each one has its own character. But because they were built in the same period, in the same region, sometimes by the same men, they all follow a similar design. Perhaps the building that represents this design at its finest is the cathedral of Notre Dame in Reims.

The city of Reims is very old, but its most loyal citizen

would not say it is beautiful. Today it is a large industrial city. The old medieval town has almost disappeared. The houses that once pressed closely against the cathedral have been swept away, and a modern avenue lined with trees leads up to it.

It was in Reims that Clovis, the ancestor of French kings, became a Christian fifteen hundred years ago. In later centuries, the kings of France were crowned in Reims cathedral. Their statues decorate the west end of the building, together with a sculpted scene of Clovis being baptized.

The present cathedral was begun after the old one was ruined by fire in about 1200. At first, the work went quickly, but the archbishop of Reims often quarreled with his subjects, the citizens of Reims. Also, Reims was in the region where French and English armies struggled during the Hundred Years' War.

These troubles slowed down the building, but the work never stopped completely. Except for the towers, the cathedral was finished before 1400. The towers took another thirty years after that, and they were not built as high as the first architect had planned.

The general shape of Reims is the same as that of most French Gothic cathedrals. At the east end is a rounded apse. The choir is high, and its vault is supported by immense flying buttresses. The transepts are rather short. They once had towers at each end, but these were destroyed by fire in 1481. The slender central spire, made of lead and timber, had to be replaced about the same time.

The west end (the main entrance, or front, of all medieval cathedrals) is especially splendid. It is unusually wide at the base, with five gables (arches that usually appear over the doors) instead of three. The shape is pleasing to the eye, and

The west front of Reims is perhaps the finest example of Gothic art in France. Compare it with the west front of Paris (page 32). The Gothic style became lighter, more slender, and more elaborate as time passed. (PHOTO CHEVOJON)

the many pinnacles and statues seem to be part of the actual building, not pieces of decoration stuck onto it.

By comparing the west front of Reims with the west front of Paris, you can see how the Gothic style developed. Paris is simpler, more solid-looking, and has less decoration. Its gables and arches are almost rounded. At Reims, the gables are more pointed. Angles everywhere are sharper. The towers, with their slender pillars, seem lighter. At Reims you experience strongly the feeling that all Gothic architecture gives you — the feeling that the building is shooting upward, toward heaven.

Reims is the most elaborate of all French Gothic cathedrals. Inside and out, it is covered with sculptures and carvings. Figures of saints, prophets, and kings march along the walls and stand in every corner. Patterns of flowers and leaves are carved along each arch and doorway. Inside the nave, splendid tapestries hang on the walls. Now, they are dusty and faded. But once they were fresh and brightly colored.

In the Middle Ages, the cathedrals were much gayer inside than they are now. The stone figures around the windows of Reims cathedral once glittered with gold. Columns were painted in colorful patterns. Through the jewel-like windows of stained glass, the light fell upon soft blues, warm reds, and glowing gold.

The paint soon faded and peeled off. And in later ages, such brilliant decoration in churches was believed to be ungodly. Many French churches (including Paris cathedral) were whitewashed. Paintings, sculptures, and gold and silver objects were taken away. Some can now be seen in museums. Other treasures, made with such care and devotion by unknown medieval artists, have disappeared forever.

Reims cathedral was luckier than Paris. While Notre Dame of Paris was damaged, ill-used, and almost wrecked during the seventeenth and eighteenth centuries, Notre Dame of Reims was not harmed. And Viollet-le-Duc, who restored Paris cathedral, also did good work at Reims.

Yet today, Reims cathedral looks badly battered. Is this just the effect of time? It is true that the building stone used for the cathedral looks chalky, but there is nothing wrong with it. No, man is to blame, and the damage is recent. In World War I, the cathedral was the target of German guns. It received several direct hits, and the roof was completely destroyed. Yet the great stone vault, below the roof, did not collapse. The cathedral-builders of medieval France did their job well.

THE CATHEDRALS OF ENGLAND

The famous Gothic cathedrals of France were built in one, rather small region. In other parts of the country, cathedrals are quite different. They are not so large, nor so beautiful. Some of them are not very interesting.

All English cathedrals have a family likeness. They are not so alike as the cathedrals of the Ile-de-France, but they are much more alike than the cathedrals of the *whole* of France. England became a nation earlier than other countries. By the time of the Norman Conquest (1066), England was already a united country under one king.

But English cathedrals did not follow a basic design, like

the French Gothic cathedrals. The medieval builders of England were practical men. Although they copied ideas from other cathedrals, they made changes of their own. French Gothic cathedrals followed a pattern — a pattern that begins in Paris, continues in Reims, and is finally carried too far in Beauvais. English cathedrals had no such basic pattern.

Also, the actual work of building took longer in England. There is not one English cathedral that was begun and finished by the same architect. Indeed, most cathedrals were under construction for two or three centuries. Lack of money was the chief reason for slow progress. It meant that the style of the building changed as it grew. If you look at the nave of Norwich cathedral, for example, you see several different styles. The bottom row of windows is Romanesque (they were built first). The next row is "Early English" (the early Gothic style in England). The next row belongs to an even later style. Almost the whole history of medieval architecture can be learned by studying just one building!

As a result of all these differences, English cathedrals are warmer and more homely than French. They have more variety and more unexpected details, but, taken all together, they are not so splendid. England has no gem of architecture like Reims cathedral. Neither does it have a heroic mistake like Beauvais.

The building of large cathedrals in England was begun by the Normans. Herbert de Losinga, the founder of Norwich cathedral, was probably a Norman. The Romanesque style of architecture is called "Norman" in England, because the Normans brought it over.

More than half the cathedrals of England were begun in Norman times. But by the time they were finished, the Gothic style had long taken over. No cathedrals that are entirely Norman now remain, although one of the most magnificent of all, Durham cathedral, is largely Norman. Standing on a cliff above a river, this splendid building shows the tremendous power of Norman architecture. It is as much a fortress as a church.

French Gothic cathedrals usually had two large towers at the west end and a small, slender spire at the center. In England the arrangement was different. Few English cathedrals have two western towers. Some have a single large tower over the west end, some have none. Instead of the slender, central spire, they have a massive tower, perhaps as wide as the nave, and sometimes carrying a spire on top. This was difficult and expensive, but the results are worth any cost.

English cathedrals often have a very long nave (see the photograph of Norwich on page 14). Also, the east end is often square, not curved like Paris and Reims. Here, the English builders saved themselves trouble — and money. A curved apse was very complicated, especially if it had large windows in it.

It is hard to pick out just one of the twenty-seven chief English cathedrals. Each building has its own virtues. There is Lincoln with its magnificent west front. There is Canterbury, headquarters of the Church of England. There is beautiful Ely, with its amazing eight-sided tower. But the cathedral that is perhaps the most splendid of all (on the outside anyway — inside it is rather dull) is Salisbury.

The majestic cathedral of Durham shares its cliff-top site with a monastery and a castle (now part of the University of Durham). English cathedrals were often built in a splendid setting. French cathedrals were usually in the town center. (A. F. KERSTING)

Salisbury cathedral, in England, stands in a close (precinct) that covers half a square mile. The close is surrounded by a wall and is entered through three medieval gates. (AEROFILMS)

Salisbury is unusual because it was built much more quickly than other English cathedrals. The body of the church was erected between 1220 and 1258 — very fast work for English builders. However, the west front was not finished until some years later, and the magnificent steeple (the tower and spire) was built around 1330. Thus, Salisbury cathedral is not a jumble of changing styles. It is a nearly perfect example of thirteenth-century English architecture.

In Norman times a cathedral was built in the nearby town of Old Sarum. In the thirteenth century, the bishop decided to build a new cathedral on a different site. Old Sarum was a military fort, and the bishop did not like having the king's soldiers as neighbors. Also, Old Sarum was built on a dry hill, and the citizens had to walk a long way to get water. So the bishop decided to build the new cathedral close to the Avon River — too close as things turned out. Salisbury cathedral has been flooded more than once.

On April 28, 1220, the bishop laid the foundation stone. Actually, he laid five stones: one for the pope, one for the archbishop of Canterbury, two for the earl and countess of Salisbury, and one for himself. Thirty-eight years later, the cathedral was almost finished.

Salisbury is the third largest cathedral in England. It is a little larger than the cathedral of Canterbury. Like Canterbury, it is in the shape of a double cross, with two sets of transepts. The roof is very high, though not as high as some French cathedrals. The stone used for the building is partly the limestone that is found nearby and partly gray marble from the west of England. Probably, the builders also used some of the stone from the old Norman cathedral of Old Sarum. Unfortunately, none of this old building is left today.

Salisbury is surrounded by acres of rich, green lawns. From whatever direction the visitor approaches, he sees the cathedral from a long distance away. The surrounding space helps to give the cathedral a clean and graceful appearance that few buildings can rival.

Salisbury's crowning glory is its tower and spire. At 404 feet, the spire is far the highest in England. Its only rival, Norwich, is nearly one hundred feet shorter. Until a very few years ago, this ancient cathedral was the highest building in England.

Once, nearly all English cathedrals had spires. Today, only Salisbury, Norwich, and two rather small ones are still standing.

When Salisbury cathedral was begun, the architect did not plan a large tower or spire. The stone piers that the tower rests on were not thick enough to carry such a weight. And it *is* a weight — about six thousand tons! So extra buttresses had to be constructed. The builders also left the wooden scaffolding in place inside the spire, to give more support.

A century later, more reinforcements were added, and in the seventeenth century, Sir Christopher Wren (the architect of St. Paul's cathedral in London) put in iron struts. In the nineteenth century, still more strengthening was needed. By that time, the spire had tilted twenty-three inches from the correct position. Architects were worried about the cathedral's foundations, for it is built on marshy ground.

Today, the cathedral authorities are again worried about their spire. It is a miracle that it has not fallen. However, it is still there, pointing toward heaven, over six hundred years after it was erected. With the help of modern engineering methods, perhaps it may last another six hundred years.

TWO GERMAN GIANTS

In Germany, the Romanesque style lasted longer than in France or England. When the Gothic style was finally introduced from France, the German builders made some changes of their own. French cathedrals usually had large towers but no spires — or very small ones like the wooden spire on Paris cathedral. But the Germans loved spires. In the rich towns of medieval Germany, spires grew taller and taller while cathedrals grew larger and larger.

The biggest church in the whole of Germany is the famous cathedral of Cologne. There was a bishop of Cologne as early as the fourth century, and in the time of Charlemagne he was made an archbishop. Cologne soon became one of the wealthiest cities in Germany, and its archbishop was a powerful man. He was not only a religious leader, but also the ruler of the city and of the land around it. He was one of the seven German princes called electors, who had the right to elect the Holy Roman Emperor.

The first stone of the present cathedral of Cologne was laid in 1248. At that time, the city was a place of violence and riots. The citizens fought against the harsh rule of the archbishop, who tried to take away their rights. With intervals of peace, the quarrel continued for more than two hundred years. It is surprising that the cathedral was ever built.

In fact, it was not finished. The medieval building had a temporary roof, and the twin towers were not begun.

Another four hundred years passed before the work was finally completed. The last stone was set in place in 1880, less than a hundred years ago. The men who finished the task, six hundred years after it was begun, tried to follow the plans of the original builders. There were some drawings to guide them. Some people think that Cologne today is the most magnificent of all Gothic cathedrals.

It is certainly large. It covers an area of 66,370 square feet, and its spires rise to the amazing height of 512 feet, more than a hundred feet higher than the spire of Salisbury. Even in modern New York, Cologne cathedral would be a tall building.

Its unusual spires are so massive that they leave no room for the big west window that other Gothic cathedrals have. But otherwise, Cologne is a fine example of Gothic architecture, with its flying buttresses and its richly decorated pinnacles. Perhaps it is a little too perfect. It does not have the spirit of the French Gothic cathedrals, which were completed in a shorter time. The lines of Cologne cathedral are so exact that they might have been worked out by a mathematician.

The spires of Cologne, mighty though they are, are not the tallest in Germany. That honor belongs to Ulm minster (a minster is a large church or cathedral, often one that once belonged to a monastery).

The citizens of Ulm in the Middle Ages were as tough and as independent as the people of Cologne. They needed to be, because Ulm was an "imperial city," with no ruler except the Holy Roman Emperor himself. They were determined to make

Cologne cathedral is the largest Gothic building in Germany. The enormous towers and spires leave no space for a round window in the center of the west front. As a result, the building looks "crowded," as if the spires are too close together. (ROGER VIOLLET)

48

The architects of medieval Germany loved very tall spires. It became common to build only one giant spire, instead of two as at Cologne. Such spires resulted from the pride of the citizens, who wanted their church to be grander than the churches of rival cities. (FRANZ STOEDTNER)

50

their church more splendid than that of any other town. They succeeded, too, although, like Cologne cathedral, Ulm minster was not finished until the nineteenth century.

Ulm minster is 464 feet long and about 50 feet wide (across the nave). It holds about 30,000 people, and in the Middle Ages the whole population of the city could easily stand inside it. Its mighty spire is 529 feet high, which makes it the tallest Gothic building in Europe.

The most important man to work on the planning of Ulm minster (and did not live to see it finished) was called Ulrich of Ensingen. He was quite young when he became the master mason at Ulm, but he was a man of determination and ambition. His skill as a builder was well-known in Europe. Once, he was invited to Italy to work on Milan cathedral, but he quarreled with his Italian colleagues and soon returned. Ulm still did not occupy all his time. He also built parts of the beautiful cathedral of Strasbourg (now in France) and several smaller German churches.

Ulrich was, perhaps, too ambitious. He was so fond of sheer size that his buildings sometimes look rather clumsy. Ulm minster was in some ways a more beautiful building before the huge spire was finally erected.

However, Ulm minster does not look top-heavy, as might be expected. The reason for this is another development of the Gothic style in Germany — the use of "openwork." Instead of solid stone sides, the steeple has spaces between the stone. It is like a string vest, compared with an ordinary T-shirt. If you look up at the towering steeple, the sky can be seen through it, which makes the building seem lighter and more graceful.

The men who erected the steeple in the nineteenth century also strengthened the roof with iron. But these additions were too much for the old brick walls to bear. Flying buttresses had to be erected, too. They look like a line of soldiers marching down the side of the building. However, they fit in well with the rest of it and do not spoil this proud monument to the independent citizens of Ulm.

MONUMENTS TO VICTORY

The cathedrals of Spain are not as famous as the cathedrals of France or England. This is surprising because, in some ways, Spanish cathedrals are the grandest of all. The cathedral of Seville, which was founded in 1402, is the largest in the world.

Early in the Middle Ages, most of Spain was conquered by Arabs, a Muslim people from North Africa. During later centuries, the Christians in Spain slowly forced the Muslims back. The last Muslim kingdom in Spain was defeated in the fifteenth century.

It was partly to celebrate their victory over the Muslims that Spanish Christians built such magnificent cathedrals.

The Muslims lived in Spain for more than seven hundred years. Although they were driven out at last, they had an important influence on Spanish art and architecture. Some Spanish cathedrals — big, square buildings with no transepts — look like Muslim mosques. The Spanish cathedral builders made delicate

Burgos cathedral, in Spain, rises from the hillside in the old city like a vast cliff. Its solid walls give it a feeling of strength, but its beautifully carved towers and pinnacles are light and graceful. (MARY ORR)

*The vault of the Constable's chapel, seen from inside, looks like a flower.
The builders of Burgos cathedral were not only skillful engineers. They
were also lovers of beauty, as this picture shows.* (MAS, BARCELONA)

patterns in brickwork. They often put in wooden ceilings, richly carved. These ideas came from Muslim architecture.

The cathedrals of Spain are museums as well as churches. Zamora cathedral has one of the richest collections of medieval tapestries in the world. They are meeting places, too, for the old traditions that have died out in other European countries still continue in Spain. The farmers of Valencia meet every Thursday on the porch of the cathedral to discuss how the water supply for the fields shall be distributed.

The Spanish cathedrals are also fortresses. They celebrate a military victory, and they still seem to offer a challenge to the world. As a ship approaches the harbor of Majorca, the magnificent cathedral of Palma is the first thing to be seen. It stands above the bay, guarding the city with its great square walls and powerful buttresses.

The cathedral of Burgos is the most striking of all Spanish cathedrals. It stands halfway up the hill on which the city of Burgos is built. The houses around it look like small boats seeking the shelter of a mighty battleship.

Burgos was once the capital of the old Spanish kingdom of Castile. It was the city of El Cid, the famous Spanish hero who lived in the eleventh century. In this century, it was the headquarters of General Francisco Franco during the Spanish Civil War. The cathedral too seems to be a center of military power. Its huge gray towers seem to threaten the sky. The steps and ramparts around it are like the approach to a castle.

Yet Burgos cathedral is not a grim building. It is saved from grimness by the lively stone decoration of its towers and walls. No less than twenty-two steeples and pinnacles rise from its towers and roof. Each one is lined with knobs, which break up its stern, straight lines. This brilliant array is the work of a remarkable family of German craftsmen who came to Burgos from Cologne.

Hans of Cologne built the two great towers on the west front. He copied the idea of openwork steeples from Cologne cathedral. Of course, the steeples of Cologne had not yet been built, but Hans had a drawing of them. This drawing later disappeared, but was found again in time to help the men who finished Cologne cathedral in the nineteenth century.

The pinnacles of the Constable's chapel at Burgos were built by Hans's son, and his grandson designed the steeples of the central tower. These additions were made in the fifteenth and sixteenth centuries, two hundred years after the cathedral was begun. But without them, Burgos cathedral would be a very ordinary building, with no special beauty.

The same richness is found inside the cathedral. Although it is rather dark, the faint light picks out stone carvings and sculptures, gold screens and painted figures. Some of the patterns are obviously borrowed from the Muslim style.

As in any old cathedral, Burgos is full of fascinating bits of history. Here is the tomb of an old constable (governor) of Castile. Carved in stone, the constable grips his sword as if waiting for an attack. Here too is the old chest, which, legend says, El Cid used to trick some greedy men. He told them that it was packed with gold, but when they opened it, it was full of sand. In the holiest chapel there is a figure of Jesus, made in wood and

The Sagrada Familia, the huge church designed by Antonio Gaudi in Barcelona, Spain, was begun nearly a hundred years ago. It still is far from finished. Gaudi planned eighteen spires for the church, rivaling the spires of Burgos. (A. F. KERSTING)

leather, with arms and legs that move. According to a story, it was made soon after the Crucifixion.

Burgos cathedral owes something to the Gothic cathedrals of France. It owes something to German and Italian architecture, and to the Muslims. Yet it has a character all its own. It is quite different from most Spanish cathedrals, which do not usually have many towers or spires. Yet it could not have been built anywhere except in Spain.

Burgos itself was the inspiration behind a modern church, the Sagrada Familia, in Barcelona. This astonishing building was designed by Antonio Gaudi and begun in 1884. It is still unfinished. Like all the buildings designed by the amazing Gaudi, the Sagrada Familia is unique. If anything, it looks more like a giant plant than a building. But its clustering spires do bring to mind the outline of Burgos cathedral, whose sparkling pinnacles rise above the bare countryside of old Castile.

CATHEDRALS OF THE KREMLIN

The Kremlin stands on a low hill in Moscow, with the Moskva River running below its walls. Five hundred years ago, when Moscow was still a small town, the Kremlin was a fortress. Moscow then was under attack from the fierce race of Tatars.

The princes of Moscow took the lead in fighting the Tatars. In about 1480, Ivan the Great succeeded in throwing off Tatar rule, and he took the title of czar. The country that he ruled was very small, compared with the size of Russia today.

Besides gaining independence for the Russian state, Ivan also declared himself the protector of all Christians who belonged to the Eastern Orthodox Church.

In the early days of the Church, Christians were divided into two groups. The Roman emperor, Constantine, who made Christianity the religion of the Roman Empire, founded a new capital city in Constantinople. While Rome became the headquarters of the Christian Church in the West, Constantinople became the headquarters of the Eastern Church.

For many centuries, East and West were divided. The two Churches grew up apart. Although Orthodox Eastern Christians believed in the same god as Roman Catholics, they really belonged to a different religion. One difference was that priests and bishops in the Orthodox Church were less influential. The patriarch of Constantinople was never as powerful a person as the pope of Rome. The rulers of the Orthodox Church, to which Russia belonged, have often been political rulers, like Ivan the Great. The chief religious leader in the Russian Church was the metropolitan (or archbishop) of Moscow. His headquarters, like the czar's, were in the Kremlin.

The Kremlin is a larger place than most visitors expect. It covers an area of about one hundred acres, and its walls stretch for about a mile and a half. Not only is it the center of the Soviet government, it is also the heart of the Russian nation. It contains cathedrals, churches, and palaces built in the time of the early czars. Nowadays, most of these buildings are museums. They are filled with marvelous treasures of Russian art, and together they create a picture of Russian history since the Middle Ages.

In the fourteenth century, four cathedrals of white stone

The cathedral of the Assumption in the Kremlin, Moscow, was once the chief Christian church of Russia. Today, it is a museum of Russian art and history. (J. ALLAN CASH)

60

were built on the south side of the Kremlin. According to old accounts, they must have looked very beautiful. But nothing of them now remains.

As Moscow grew, new buildings were added, and old ones pulled down. The white stone cathedrals were too small for the capital city of a great nation. In the fifteenth and sixteenth centuries, the Kremlin was almost entirely rebuilt.

One of the buildings constructed at this time was the cathedral of the Assumption. It was the chief Russian church, and contained the throne of the metropolitan of Moscow. In it are the tombs of all the metropolitans down to 1700. The czars once were crowned in the cathedral, and important acts of state were announced from it.

When it was first built, it was the largest building in the area. Nowadays, it does not look especially large, perhaps because a large modern building has been put up near it, spoiling the view from the southwest.

The architect was an Italian, but the cathedral of the Assumption looks more Russian than Italian. It is an almost square building of white stone. The roof is rounded, to form four arches on the longer sides and two on the shorter sides. Up to roof level, it might just be an odd variation of a classical Italian building. But when the spectator raises his eyes above the roof, he knows he is in Russia.

Like many Russian churches, the cathedral of the Assumption is topped by five domes. They are gilded, and glisten brightly in the sun, especially if there is snow on the ground. Each dome is placed on a stone drum, to make it higher, and the central dome is larger than the other four. Against a pale blue Russian sky, they make a splendid sight.

Inside, the cathedral is beautifully decorated with wall paintings. The roof is supported by slender pillars, which are also covered with paintings of saints and other figures. The architect was very skillful with the ceiling. Looking upward from inside, all the domes are the same size. But from the outside, the central dome is larger.

There are several other fine churches in the Kremlin, but the most famous of all was built just outside it, in Red Square. This is the astonishing cathedral of St. Basil, built in the middle of the sixteenth century.

The buildings of the Kremlin are splendid and stately, but rather stern. The walls that surround them are powerful and grim. But St. Basil's cathedral is a joyful, fantastic building. The Kremlin seems to say: life is serious, life is hard. Across the square, St. Basil's cathedral replies: life is glorious, life is happy.

Seen from the other side of Red Square, St. Basil's is a great cluster of steeples, turrets, and domes, swirling upward together. The main towers look a little like huge fruits — pineapples, melons, lemons. They are all different, yet they seem to match each other perfectly. The cathedral is built mainly of white and red stone, and the curves and angles are outlined in blue and white. The topmost dome of all, which is perched on a steeple like the satellite on the nose of a space rocket, is gilded. All the domes end in a sparkling white cross. If Walt Disney had been a great architect instead of a cartoonist, he might have designed a building like St. Basil's cathedral.

Splendid St. Basil's gives a joyful air to Red Square in Moscow, which is not otherwise a very joyful-looking place. Many of Moscow's historic buildings were designed by foreign architects, but St. Basil's is a fine example of a Russian national architecture. (J. ALLAN CASH)

The cathedral of Masasi, in Tanzania, was founded as a British missionary church. It is the headquarters of a diocese that is larger than England.
(UNITED SOCIETY FOR THE PROPAGATION OF THE GOSPELS)

64

AN AFRICAN CATHEDRAL

In the southeast of the republic of Tanzania, there is a hill called Mtandi, which rises about three thousand feet above sea level. Halfway up one side is a large, stone building, with a gabled front like an old Dutch house. Near roof level, there is a large round opening, like an eye, which looks toward the center of Africa. This is the cathedral of Masasi.

The first Christian priests came to Masasi nearly one hundred years ago. They were British missionaries from Zanzibar, and they came to start a mission among the people who live in this corner of Tanzania. Many of the Africans became Christian, but the missionaries were not liked by everyone. In 1882, their little church was raided and destroyed.

At about this time, Tanzania came under German rule. The coming of Europeans made the violence that already existed in this part of Africa even worse. But the mission at Masasi continued to grow, and new missions were started in the villages nearby. An English architect came to supervise the building of a stone church. Stonemasons were hired from Zanzibar to teach the people the craft of stonecutting. Until then, all the buildings were made of mud or wood. Luckily, good granite was discovered in the hill of Mtandi itself, and in June, 1905, the first stone was laid by the bishop of Zanzibar.

Soon afterward, another disaster struck the mission. A rebellion broke out against all foreigners in the Masasi region, and the church and other buildings of the mission were destroyed. The work had to begin all over again, but in 1909, the church was almost finished. It was dedicated to the saints Mary and Bartholomew.

The church of Masasi had many more trials to go through before it became a cathedral. Some of the priests were suspended from their duties·for bad behavior. Later, during World War I, the priests of Masasi, both British and African, were jailed by the German authorities. Some of them were put to work in chain gangs, and more than one died under this treatment.

After the war, Tanzania came under British rule, and the work at Masasi was restarted. Many new churches were built in other villages. So many, in fact, that in 1926 Masasi was made a new diocese. The church became a cathedral, and the first bishop of Masasi was created.

Three years later, the cathedral was enlarged. The west front was built at this time, and wooden carvings were made for it by African craftsmen. The bishop's throne was also carved from Masasi wood. At last, the cathedral was finished.

The cost of building it was not great, yet it is large and impressive with massive stone pillars and a long nave. Its narrow windows let in enough light — but not too much of the hot African sun. The roof is made of corrugated iron, which does not last very long. And when it rains, neither the voice of the priest nor the notes of the organ can be heard above the clatter of rain on the iron roof.

When it was built, it was the only stone church in the diocese. Fire and cyclones, which destroy so many buildings in tropical Africa, cannot do serious damage to the cathedral of Masasi. Perhaps it may last as long as the medieval cathedrals of Europe.

SPIRES AMONG THE SKYSCRAPERS

The great age of cathedral-building in Europe ended during the Middle Ages. Of course, other cathedrals were built later. Some of the most famous cathedrals and churches, like St. Peter's in Rome or St. Paul's in London, were built after the Gothic period had ended. But between the fifteenth and the nineteenth centuries, the number of new cathedrals built was rather small.

In the nineteenth century, a new age of cathedral-building began. This was a time of religious revival. Populations were growing, and more churches were needed. New bishops were created to serve the growing industrial cities. Old churches were "promoted" to be cathedrals, and some completely new cathedrals were built as well.

Most of the new buildings were built in the Gothic style. During the nineteenth century, men became fascinated by the Middle Ages. That distant period seemed invitingly peaceful and simple. There was a revival of interest in medieval art. Henry Adams, the famous American scholar, was one of many who became interested in the Gothic art of the Middle Ages. He wrote a great book about the religious art of medieval France, called *Mont Saint-Michel and Chartres*. So it was not surprising that new churches were built in the Gothic style. In fact, the "Gothic revival" was not limited to religious buildings. Hotels, railroad stations, and most other kinds of buildings were designed in the nineteenth-century version of Gothic.

The fastest-growing country in the nineteenth century was

the United States, and many of its new citizens were Roman Catholics. That meant more bishops and more cathedrals. America became the greatest cathedral builder among Western nations in the nineteenth century.

The first Roman Catholic Mass celebrated in New York was probably as early as 1683. But Roman Catholics in New York had no church of their own for more than a hundred years after that. For a time, the Roman Catholic religion was banned by the British colonial authorities, and the Mass was celebrated in an old loft.

The first church was built in 1786 and, twenty-nine years later, the first cathedral of St. Patrick rose on a lot in the south of Manhattan. Shortly after that the Roman Catholic Church purchased another lot, on Fifth Avenue, for a college. The college was never built, but in 1850, the archbishop of New York suggested that the site should be used for a new cathedral. An architect was hired to draw up plans.

The man appointed was an American architect and engineer named James Renwick. Although he was still a young man, he was already an experienced church architect. At the age of twenty-four, he had won a competition to design the charming Grace Church that now stands on Broadway and 10th Street, in Manhattan.

James Renwick was one of the first leaders of the "Gothic revival" in America. He had seen and admired the medieval

St. Patrick's cathedral stands on Fifth Avenue in New York City. It is built in the style of French Gothic cathedrals of the fourteenth century. Nowadays, it is difficult to get a good view of this attractive cathedral because taller buildings surround it on all sides. (C. HARRISON CONROY COMPANY)

68

This photograph shows the nave of St. Patrick's, looking toward the west door. Over the door are the pipes of one of the two organs. Above them is the rose window, which measures 26 feet across. (RELIGIOUS NEWS SERVICE PHOTO)

cathedrals of Europe, and in the new St. Patrick's he showed how well he had understood the lessons of the medieval builders. He skillfully reproduced the effect of Gothic architecture, but he was not afraid of using modern methods. Medieval cathedrals were constructed on a frame of rough wooden beams. They were held together by stone and cement. Renwick, who was a trained engineer as well as an architect, was able to use methods unknown to the medieval builders. The stone for St. Patrick's was cut by machines, and the walls arose on a frame of powerful iron girders.

St. Patrick's has a look of several medieval cathedrals, especially Cologne and Reims. But it is not exactly like either. Although the style is not new, the building itself is unique. It is a fine example of an ancient tradition renewed through the imagination of a new generation.

Under the surface, Manhattan is made of natural rock. (That is why tall skyscrapers can be built there easily.) The foundations of St. Patrick's consist of enormous granite blocks, fitted into the natural rock. The base of the walls is also granite, and the surface, or facing, is made of white marble from a quarry in New York State. Behind this layer of marble, the walls are made of rougher stone. They are over twelve feet thick, and contain hollow spaces to prevent dampness. Although the city air has turned the marble dark gray in places, the walls are well constructed. No cracks have yet appeared.

Like most Gothic cathedrals, St. Patrick's is in the form of a cross. At the west end are twin towers, topped by spires. They rise 330 feet above the street. Between them, over the main door, is a magnificent rose window. Like a great colored wheel, it lets dimly shaded light into the nave. There are seats for more than

71

three thousand people, and for important occasions, nearly twice as many can stand inside without feeling crowded.

The cornerstone of the cathedral was laid in 1858. Work came to a stop during the Civil War, but by 1879 the main body of the cathedral was complete. The spires were finished in 1888. Medieval builders would have been amazed at such speed.

James Renwick died in 1895, and a few remaining parts were added after his death. The Lady chapel, at the east end, was not built until 1906. It was designed by a different architect, who followed an earlier Gothic style, but it fits in well with the rest of the cathedral.

St. Patrick's is not among the ten largest Gothic cathedrals, but it is bigger than most European cathedrals. It is 332 feet long and 174 feet wide, and it takes up a whole city block. It covers an area of 4,674 square yards, which is larger than a football field.

When it was first built, St. Patrick's cathedral was a splendid landmark. Its lofty spires, which far outreached the buildings round about, could be seen from miles away. Now, all is changed. Someone walking along crowded Fifth Avenue today might almost pass by the cathedral without noticing it. It is easily lost among the colorful windows of the department stores. Its once-lofty spires are dwarfed by the huge towers of Rockefeller Center, on the other side of Fifth Avenue.

Yet "St. Pat's" is still a landmark for New Yorkers. Among the stores and offices, it keeps its own dignity. The crowds who go on tours of the television studios in Rockefeller Center are not much larger than the crowds who come to worship, or to watch, in St. Patrick's, the most famous Roman Catholic church in the United States.

A HOUSE OF PRAYER
FOR ALL PEOPLE

Italy has St. Peter's, Rome. France has Notre Dame of Paris. England has Westminster Abbey. George Washington, the first president of the United States, wanted his country also to have a great national church. He spoke hopefully of building one. But for over a hundred years his hope was unfulfilled.

In 1893, Congress granted a charter "to establish and maintain within the District of Columbia a cathedral. . . ." Fourteen years later, the cornerstone was laid by President Theodore Roosevelt. The constitution of the cathedral stated that it was to be a "House of Prayer for all people, for ever free and open, welcoming all who enter its doors."

The national cathedral in Washington is dedicated to St. Peter and St. Paul. Although it was founded by Protestants belonging to the Episcopal Church, it serves as a truly national church — a "House of Prayer for all people." Today, many different groups worship there. Services are conducted not only by Episcopalians in Washington, but also by Russian Orthodox, Jewish, and several other congregations

The building is not yet finished. When work began in 1907, the builders estimated that it would take seventy-eight years. But it may take a little longer than that.

Seventy-eight years to put up one building? That seems very slow. A fifty-storey office block can be finished in two years. Why should the national cathedral take such a long time?

Of course the medieval cathedrals took much longer. Even Paris, which was built faster than most, was far from complete a hundred years after it was begun. Washington cathedral is

Gothic, and a Gothic cathedral is much more difficult to build than a modern office tower. It is true that the builders can take advantage of modern materials — steel girders instead of wood, for example. But the cathedral has been built, as far as possible, in the manner of medieval builders. The same care and love have gone into it.

St. Patrick's cathedral in New York is descended from French and German Gothic buildings. But Washington looks more like an English cathedral. From a distance, it reminds Englishmen of such great cathedrals as Durham or York.

Some people do not admire modern Gothic architecture, but nobody can deny that Washington cathedral is a spendid building. It dominates the city skyline, along with the Capitol and the Washington Monument. It was designed to be the most magnificent church in North America, and many people say that it is.

The cathedral is lucky to have a fine, spacious site. It stands on the top of Mount St. Albans, the highest point in the city. Smooth, wide lawns make a rich carpet for its massive walls. Beautiful trees and flowers are planted around it. The towers rise high above the city, a hundred feet higher than the Washington Monument (which is, however, built on lower ground).

Washington cathedral is about one-tenth of a mile long and covers an area almost the size of two football fields. That makes it the sixth largest Gothic cathedral in the world. The largest of all is the unfinished cathedral of St. John the Divine, in New York City.

The national cathedral is being built stone by stone. It is not just a copy of an old building, although it is in an old style. Some new buildings built in a style of the past can look dull and

The cathedral of St. Peter and St. Paul in Washington, D.C., is a national shrine as well as a church. Every Sunday, one of the fifty states is honored here, and special prayers are said for the people of the state. (WASHINGTON CATHEDRAL PHOTO)

lifeless. They do not seem to have any feeling. They might have been designed by computers.

This is not true of Washington cathedral. Inside its splendid nave, there is an atmosphere of richness and pride. This is a national shrine, as well as a church. The figures in the stained-glass windows are American heroes as well as Christian saints. There is a fine statue of George Washington, much better than most of the statues of the first president that are scattered across the country.

Even more striking is the kneeling statue of Abraham Lincoln, by Herbert Honck of Harrisburg, Pennsylvania. Of all the thousands of Lincoln statues throughout the world, this is probably the only one that shows him kneeling. There is a reason. The sculptor's grandfather was walking through the country near Gettysburg, soon after the great Civil War battle. He came upon President Lincoln all alone, kneeling in prayer in a field. The sculptor remembered his grandfather's story when he came to make his statue.

Nowadays, there are few craftsmen who have the talents of the workers on medieval cathedrals. It was difficult to find carvers and stonemasons for Washington cathedral. Only about twelve men in the United States possess these old skills, and many of them are probably descended from the families who worked on medieval cathedrals. A hundred years from now, there may be nobody left who can do the kind of work needed for a building like Washington cathedral.

It is taking a long time to build the cathedral. But when it is finished, it should stand for a far longer time. Experts say that it should last for three thousand years. Let us hope that fire, bombs, or air pollution do not prove them wrong.

CATHEDRALS OF
TODAY—AND TOMORROW

The last true Gothic churches were built in the fifteenth century. For many years after that, Gothic architecture was out of fashion. Most Protestants, and many Roman Catholics, too, disliked it. Gothic cathedrals were badly treated. Then came the nineteenth-century revival. The old cathedrals were cleaned and restored. Scholars began to study them. The loving skill of the medieval builders was at last understood and respected. New cathedrals, like St. Patrick's, were built in Gothic style.

But why did nineteenth-century architects copy a medieval style?

Above all, the influence of Paris and Reims, of Salisbury and Cologne, was very strong. Those Gothic cathedrals were the most splendid creations of European architecture. Many people believed that Gothic was the only style suitable for a cathedral. No other style would do.

Nowadays, ideas have changed again. Gothic cathedrals are still admired, but none is being started. Probably, no cathedral will ever be built again in the Gothic style.

Most Christians today believe that their Church must enter into the lives of ordinary people. The Church should be a part of our own time. Churches and cathedrals should not be memorials to an age that has passed. If its buildings are old-fashioned, people will think that the Christian religion is old-fashioned, too. A church should be as up-to-date as a movie theater or a supermarket.

Modern architects do not like to design buildings that belong to the past. They believe that the *function* of a building (what it does) is more important than what it looks like. The first question that modern architects ask is: What is the building for? If the building is designed to do its job well, then it will probably look good, too.

Before he starts his plans, the architect of any building must know what is going to happen inside it. If he is designing an office building, he must know what office workers do and what they need. The most beautiful office building in the world is no good at all if the clerks have to take a five-minute walk to the coffee machine.

An architect who is designing a church or a cathedral must ask himself the same questions. What is going to happen inside the church? What do the people need?

If he answers these questions honestly, he will never design a Gothic church. A Gothic church is really very inconvenient. Because it is long and narrow, many people have to sit a long way from the altar. If they are behind a pillar, they cannot even see the altar. In the Middle Ages, processions were often held in cathedrals. A long, narrow nave was useful then. But today, processions play a very small part in church services.

A church, like an office building or a sports stadium, must *function* well. Yet a church *is* different from other kinds of buildings. It is not only a building for people, it is also a house of God. Christians want their church to look like a house of God. They are not happy if it looks like a railroad station or a public library. And a cathedral, the bishop's headquarters, must be larger and more splendid than an ordinary church.

So church architects today have a difficult problem. The Gothic style has been ruled out, but no other style has replaced

The grain elevators of Kansas wheat farms influenced the design of the cathedral in Salina. (CATHEDRAL OF THE SACRED HEART PHOTO)

This photograph shows two very different modern cathedrals in Liverpool, England. The new Roman Catholic cathedral is circular. It looks like a shimmering crown, or perhaps a spacecraft ready to be launched. Inside, the altar is in the center of the building, and the congregation sits in a circle round it. In the background is the Anglican (Protestant) cathedral, designed in the Gothic style. It was begun in the nineteenth century and is not yet finished. (ELSAM, MANN & COOPER LTD.)

it. Many new ideas have been tried in modern churches. Some are very simple. Some are very elaborate. All are different.

Some modern churches reflect the way of life of the people who worship in them. In this way, the everyday affairs of men and women are made part of their religious worship. There is a good example of such a building in Kansas.

Kansas is a wheat-growing region. Wherever you look, there are fields and farms. On every farm, rising above the fields, are tall, round buildings standing in a tidy row. They are grain elevators, used for storing grain. If Kansas was to choose a new state symbol, a grain elevator might be a suitable choice.

In fact, that is what has happened in the cathedral of the Sacred Heart in Salina, Kansas. The cathedral takes the grain elevator as a symbol. Tall, drumlike shapes run along its walls and around its tower. If the cathedral were in another state, its design might seem peculiar. But in Kansas, it is easy to guess where the design came from. Medieval cathedrals have windows or carvings showing scenes from everyday life. The cathedral in Salina has taken this idea a step further.

A different kind of symbol can be seen in the First Presbyterian Church of Stamford, Connecticut. The sanctuary (the east end) there is shaped like a fish. In the early years of Christianity, when Christians were being persecuted in Rome, a fish was their secret sign. They drew it on the walls of the caves where they hid from the Roman soldiers. However, the sign of the fish does not have any deep meaning today. The Presbyterians in Stamford do not have to hide in caves!

One of the most famous cathedrals that has been built since World War II is the cathedral of Coventry, in England. Coventry is an industrial city in the center of England. During

World War II, it was a target for German bombing raids, and the old cathedral of St. Michael, built in the fifteenth century, was destroyed.

The church authorities decided to build a new cathedral, next to the ruins of the old one. The tower and some part of the walls of the old cathedral were still standing. They were carefully repaired, to stand as a memorial to the medieval builders and a reminder of the evil of war.

Sir Basil Spence, the architect at Coventry, was faced with a difficult problem. He had to design a building that would fit in well with the ruins of the old Gothic cathedral. But the new building also had to represent the modern city of Coventry, a city of office towers, apartment buildings and factories.

Although it is built in a modern style, Coventry cathedral follows the tradition of the medieval architects. We sometimes forget that Gothic architecture did not stand still. It was continually changing and developing. There is a great difference between a twelfth-century cathedral and a fifteenth-century one.

The new cathedral in Coventry is very tall, but it has no large tower or spire (which would clash with the tower of the old cathedral). The walls are not straight, but follow a zigzag pattern of angles. One side of each angle is solid stone. The other side is stained glass, making a huge window from floor to roof. From one point of view, only windows can be seen; from the opposite point of view, only stone walls, which give the building a look of great strength.

At the entrance, wide steps lead up to a porch with a strange, curved roof. Next to the entrance is a large bronze sculpture of "St. Michael and the Devil," specially made for the cathedral of St. Michael by Sir Jacob Epstein.

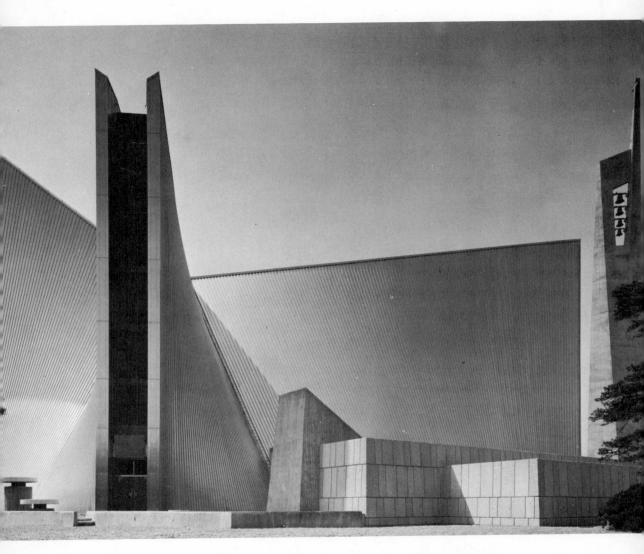

This cathedral is in Tokyo, Japan. It was designed by the brilliant modern architect Kenzo Tange. He has made solid slabs of concrete look light and delicate. (Y. FUTAGAWA)

The new cathedral of Coventry, in England, is attached to the ruins of the old building, which was destroyed during World War II. The old Gothic steeple can be seen on the left. (THOMPSON, COVENTRY)

Inside, the cathedral is filled with a warm light. It contains many beautiful objects, made by different artists. Perhaps the most famous is the tapestry (a picture woven like a carpet) that hangs behind the altar. It shows the figure of Christ, with hands raised in blessing, against a background of green and gold. It was designed by the well-known British artist Graham Sutherland, and it is the larget tapestry in the world.

In nearly all Christian churches, the altar is in the east end. This is a very old tradition. It goes back to the earliest churches, when Christianity was struggling against pagan religions. Probably, the altar was placed in the east to please the people who worshiped the sun — which rises in the east.

Coventry cathedral had to be built at right angles to the old cathedral. It runs from north to south, instead of east to west. Therefore, the altar is in the north, which breaks the old tradition. But nobody in Coventry worships the sun nowadays!

Many people do not like Coventry's new cathedral. Some think it is too modern. Others think it is too "traditonal." It is hard to please everyone. The church authorities in Coventry believe that their new cathedral is a splendid and successful mixture of old and new.

But Coventry has not set a new style for cathedrals. When a new Roman Catholic cathedral was built a few years ago in Liverpool, which is not far from Coventry, a completely different plan was chosen. And neither Coventry nor Liverpool is a guide to the future.

What will cathedrals look like a hundred years from now? No one can say for certain. Modern architects have many different ideas. Builders have many new materials. We shall probably see great variety among the cathedrals of the future. There will be no basic design like the Gothic plan in France. Each cathedral will be planned to suit the city where it is built.

Maybe no new cathedrals will be undertaken in a hundred years' time. That is a possibility, but we must hope it does not come true. For cathedrals in the past have been among man's finest artistic creations. They still have a part to play in our society.

INDEX

ABOUT THE AUTHOR

Neil Grant was born, raised, and educated in England. After receiving a master's degree in history from Cambridge University, he emigrated to the United States, where he taught school and worked for several years as an editor. While in America, Mr. Grant began his career as a writer of books for young people. At present, he is back in England, writing full time. Among Mr. Grant's other books are: *Benjamin Disraeli, Charles V, Victoria: Queen and Empress, The Renaissance* (A First Book), and *Munich: 1938*, all published by Franklin Watts, Inc.